CHICKEN

CHICKEN RECIPES FOR THE ADVENTUROUS COOK

CHICKEN

CHICKEN RECIPES FOR
THE ADVENTUROUS COOK

Quantum
Books

A QUANTUM BOOK

Published by
Quantum Books Ltd
6 Blundell Street
London N7 9BH

1-86160-187-5

Project Manager: Rebecca Kingsley
Designer: Bruce Low
Editor: Sarah Harris

The material in this publication previously appeared in
The Chicken Cookbook and *The Complete
Chicken Cookbook*

QUMCHKN
Set in Fritz Quadrata
Reproduced in Singapore by Eray Scan
Printed in Singapore by Star Standard Industries (Pte) Ltd

Contents

····

INTRODUCTION

6

SOUPS AND STARTERS

10

HOT AND SPICY

16

RICE AND PASTA

32

ROASTS, STEWS AND CASSEROLES

48

INTRODUCTION

Chicken is one of the most widespread sources of food in the world, and has been so since chickens were first domesticated thousands of years ago.

With almost all countries boasting at least one chicken dish among their traditional  national recipes, such global popularity must surely be due as much to the versatility of chicken as well as to its ready availability and relative cheapness.

Roasted, boiled, marinated or served with a sauce, chicken can be cooked in a variety of ways to tempt every palate, from the adventurous to the traditional.

Yet as well as being economical, plentiful and versatile, chicken also offers an extra bonus. High in protein and vitamins, but low in cholesterol, it also meets the nutritional requirements of today's health-conscious society.

The flavour of any chicken dish depends on the kind of chicken you use, and this flavour in turn depends in the age of the bird, and its method of rearing.

Poussins are baby chickens, weighing up to 900g (2lb). They are not full of flavour, but are ideal for barbecuing.

Broilers are immature birds which weigh in at around 1.1-1.5 Kg (2.5-3.5lb) These are very tender and are particularly suitable for any recipe that calls for chicken to be grilled or fried.

Roasting chickens are around 1.8 - 2.2 kg (4-5lb) and contain the most flavour, although cooking times will be longer to get the full taste benefit. Large roasters

can also be bought, which are ideal for traditional family roasts.

Boiling fowl are the toughest old birds and are ideally suited for long, slow casseroling.

Capons are cockerels which have been injected with hormones as a neutering agent. They are specially bred to produce a meaty roast.

Corn-fed chickens are specially reared on a diet of maize grains. This enhances their flavour, as well as giving them a distinctive yellowish skin tone.

Ill-prepared or undercooked chicken can be common causes of food-poisoning from bacteria such as salmonella. As well as ensuring that chicken is always completely cooked, it is equally important to take some care in choosing and storing chicken before use.

When picking a fresh chicken, ensure that the skin has a healthy, pinkish tone, and always check the sell-by date carefully. Ready-frozen chickens should be transported to your freezer as quickly as possible, to avoid any danger of partial defrosting. If you are freezing a fresh bird, always follow the freezing instructions carefully. A whole chicken should remain frozen for no longer than three months, and if you are freezing cooked chicken, this reduces to two months. It is also important to remember that cooked chicken should never be reheated, as this again can lead to bacterial poisoning.

When defrosting frozen chicken, you must always ensure that the bird is completely unfrozen before cooking. As a guide, a 900g (2lb) chicken requires 8 hours to defrost thoroughly at room temperature, and 28 hours if defrosting in a refrigerator, while a 3.1 kg (7lb) chicken will need 16 hours at room temperature, or 56 hours in a refrigerator.

There are many ways of cooking chicken, but the four most popular methods are roasting, casseroling, broiling and frying.

The general rule for roasting is to allow 20 minutes per 450g (1lb), plus 20 minutes extra for a bird of 1.8Kg (4lb) or under. A larger chicken should be given 5 minutes extra per lb. Oven temperature should be 190°C/375°F/Gas mark 5. If chicken is stuffed, a further 20-25 minutes cooking time should be added. As chicken has a very low fat content, it can dry out quite easily. One method of preventing this is to lay bacon strips across the bird, which should be removed for the last 20 minutes of cooking time to allow the chicken to brown. Wrapping the chicken in foil will also help retain the chicken's natural juices. In this case, allow an extra 15 minutes cooking time.

it is always important that chicken is cooked thoroughly. The easiest and safest way of doing this is to pierce the thickest part of the thigh with a knife or skewer. When the juices run clear, the bird is cooked.

Casseroling or pot roasting involves oven cooking the chicken with a sauce or stock in a sealed dish. The cooking time is generally longer than roasting, but the advantage of this is that even the toughest old chickens become succulent and tender.

Before placing in the casserole, the chicken should be sealed over a high heat to retain as many of the juices as possible.

There are a variety of ways of frying a  chicken, some more health-conscious than others! Deep-fat frying is the most fattening, and care must be taken to ensure the oil temperature is just right. Too cool and the batter will absorb the oil, and become greasy rather than crisp. Too hot, and the outside will crisp and brown before the chicken inside is cooked. Sautéing is most often used to seal chicken before casseroling. Along with stir-frying, it is the healthiest way to enjoy fried chicken, as the speed of cooking means that less oil is absorbed.

Broiling is a very similar method to roasting, but requires a little more attention. Rather than being inside an oven, the chicken is exposed to heat from one direction - say for example a barbecue. Although quicker than roasting, care must be taken to turn the bird frequently to prevent it burning or drying out.

Alternative methods for cooking chicken include steaming, poaching or using a microwave oven - something that can also be successfully used to defrost a frozen chicken. Microwave ovens vary in wattage, and it is important to follow the manufacturer's instructions carefully.

Whichever method of cooking you employ, there will be an almost bewildering array of dishes to choose between. The recipes in this book have been chosen to provide the most delicious selection of nutritionally well-balanced and truly mouth-watering dishes from around the world.

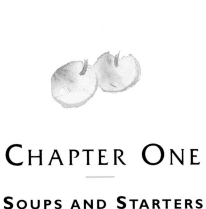

CHAPTER ONE

SOUPS AND STARTERS

QUENELLES OF CHICKEN
WITH SORREL SAUCE

■

CHICKEN, PRAWN
AND SWEETCORN CHOWDER

■

LEMON CHICKEN SOUP

■

CHICKEN PHO

QUENELLES OF CHICKEN WITH SORREL SAUCE
SERVES 4

INGREDIENTS

375 g (13 oz) chicken breast, skinned
1 egg plus 1 egg white
125 ml (4 fl oz) fromage frais or double cream
salt and freshly ground pepper
15 ml (1 tbsp) fresh chives, chopped
1.25 l (2 pt) chicken stock

Sauce

250 g (8 oz) sorrel leaves
375 ml (12 fl oz) chicken stock
60 ml (4 tbsp) fromage frais
salt and freshly ground black pepper

Garnish

fresh chives

Quenelles are small, egg-shapes of a mousse-like, finely minced meat mixture, poached in a simmering liquid. The quenelle mixture can be prepared in advance, but must be cooked at the very last moment. Vary the sauce according to the availability of fresh herbs. Tarragon, mixed herbs, even watercress, are equally good.

Cut up the chicken and put it into a food processor and work until finely chopped.

Season, add the egg and egg white and process again until smooth. Fold in the fromage frais and chives. Adjust the seasoning, turn onto a wetted plate and chill for 3–4 hours.

Meanwhile, make the sauce. Remove the larger stalks from the sorrel and blanch the leaves in 125 ml (4 fl oz) of boiling stock. Allow to cool, then purée in a liquidizer together with the fromage frais. Season to taste.

Boil the remaining stock until reduced by half. Stir into the sorrel sauce, and keep warm.

To make the quenelles, mould the chilled chicken into oval shapes by using 2 wet dessertspoons. Bring the 1.2 l (2 pt) of stock to a simmer in a large frying pan. Gently slide each quenelle into the simmering stock and poach for about 2 minutes on each side. Drain on absorbent kitchen paper towels.

Spoon the warmed sauce onto 4 individual plates, top with the quenelles and garnish with fresh chives. Serve immediately.

CHICKEN, PRAWN & SWEETCORN CHOWDER

SERVES 4 TO 6

INGREDIENTS

30 ml (2 tbsp) vegetable oil

2 medium onions, finely chopped

2 medium potatoes, peeled and diced

2 pinches grated nutmeg

750 ml (1¼ pt) chicken stock (broth)

salt and freshly ground black pepper

50 g (2 oz) streaky smoked bacon, derinded and chopped

1 boneless chicken breast (approx. 150 g / 5 oz) skinned and sliced in strips

1 small can (approx. 225 g (7 oz)) sweetcorn kernels, drained

125 g (4 oz) peeled prawns (shrimp) (or 4 scallops, chopped)

300 ml (½ pt) milk

60 ml (4 tbsp) single cream or fromage frais

freshly chopped chervil to garnish

A meal on its own. The word 'chowder' derives from the French Canadian cooking utensil. 'Chaudière'. Originally Newfoundland fishermen made a stew of cod and potatoes, but the recipe developed to include clams, scallops and salmon. In this version, I hope I am forgiven for introducing chicken to the 'chaudière'. The combination marries well and makes the expensive shellfish ingredients go further.

Heat the oil in a large saucepan and cook the onions for 10 minutes, or until softened, but not browned. Add the diced potato and nutmeg and cook for a further 5 minutes. Stir in the stock, cover and simmer for 15 minutes. Purée in a liquidizer. Season to taste.

Fry the bacon in its own fat until well browned. Add the chicken and cook for a further 2 minutes. Stir in the sweetcorn kernels, and prawns (shrimp) or scallops. Add the puréed stock mixture and blend in the milk. Simmer gently for 10 minutes or until the chicken is tender. Season to taste.

Serve in deep bowls, garnished with a swirl of cream (or fromage frais) and a dusting of chopped chervil. Accompany with crusty brown bread.

LEMON CHICKEN SOUP
SERVES 4

INGREDIENTS

1.3–1.75 kg (3–4 lb) free-range chicken, cut into pieces

750 ml (1¼ pt) chicken stock

1 medium onion, chopped

2 large beef tomatoes, peeled, seeded and chopped

15 ml (1 tbsp) fresh tarragon leaves

5 ml (1 tsp) grated lemon peel

salt and freshly ground pepper

2 Cyprus potatoes, peeled and chopped

225 g (8 oz) okra, topped and tailed

50 g (2 oz) canned chopped jalapeño chillies

100 g (4 oz) frozen sweetcorn kernels

juice of 1 lemon

Garnish
chopped flat-leaved parsley

paprika

Chickens in the peasant areas of Lebanon are very much free range and, since they are valued for their eggs, can live to a ripe age (for a chicken!). Older hens find their way into soups like this one.

In a large casserole, combine the chicken pieces (except for the breasts), the stock, onion, tomatoes, tarragon and peel. Pour over 3 cups of water, season to taste, and bring to the boil. Reduce the heat, cover and simmer for 20 minutes. Add the breasts and continue to cook until the breasts are just cooked through. Remove all the chicken pieces from the soup with a slotted spoon and set them aside to cool.

Add the potatoes to the soup, cover and continue to simmer until the potatoes are done, about 25 minutes; add the okra after 10 minutes.

When the chicken is cool enough to handle, remove the meat from the bones, discarding the skin. Chop the meat into small pieces. Add to the soup, together with the chillies and corn kernels. Bring the soup back to the boil, reduce the heat, and simmer for 5 more minutes. Stir in the lemon juice and serve immediately, garnished with chopped parsley and paprika to taste.

CHICKEN PHO
SERVES 4

INGREDIENTS

3 celery sticks, finely chopped

3 spring onions (scallions), chopped into rings (use green tops as well)

275 g (10 oz) cooked chicken, finely shredded

225 g (8 oz) flour sticks or spaghetti noodles

900 ml (1½ pt) chicken stock or use good-quality bouillon cube

2 pieces light wood ear fungus or 8 white button mushrooms, finely sliced

Traditionally, pho was only made with beef. However, it was recently spotted in Saigon being made with chicken and prawns. The light wood ear fungi are very nutritious and said to be good for the spirit.

Place the celery and spring onions (scallions) in a bowl and put on the table. Place the cooked shredded chicken in a separate bowl and put that on the table also.

Follow the instructions on the flour sticks pack, or boil up the spaghetti until just soft. Drain and rinse with some boiling water. Place in 4 bowls.

Boil up the chicken stock until simmering, then add the light wood ear fungus or the mushrooms. Place in a bowl and put on the table.

The guests should put a mixture of celery, spring onion, and shredded chicken onto the noodles then ladle the hot chicken broth into the bowls.

CHAPTER TWO

HOT AND SPICY

GINGERED CHICKEN WITH HONEY

■

SPICED BEAN CHICKEN

■

BASIL FRIED CHICKEN

■

TROPICAL STIR-FRY

■

CHICKEN KASHMIR

■

SPANISH CHICKEN WITH
TOMATOES, PEPPER AND CUMIN

■

CHICKEN WITH SPRING ONIONS

■

RED CHICKEN CURRY

■

YAKITORI CHICKEN SKEWERS

■

TANGY LIME JUICE AND
GARLIC CHICKEN WINGS

GINGERED CHICKEN WITH HONEY

SERVES 4

INGREDIENTS

30 ml (2 tbsp) sunflower oil

4 chicken breasts, skinned and part-boned, approx. 175 g (6 oz) each

5 cm (2 in) root ginger, peeled and cut into tiny matchsticks

2 medium onions, peeled and sliced

10 ml (2 tsp) ground ginger

60 ml (4 tbsp) light soy sauce

60 ml (4 tbsp) dry sherry

30 ml (2 tbsp) clear honey

salt and freshly ground black pepper

Garnish

3 spring onions (scallions) trimmed and finely chopped

This dish is very simply prepared and best accompanied with pilau rice.

Heat the oil in a pan and sauté the chicken pieces until golden.

Add the fresh ginger and onions to the oil and sauté until the onions soften. Stir in the ground ginger and cook for a further 2 minutes.

Return the chicken to the pan and cook for a minute more, then pour on the soy sauce, dry sherry and honey.

Cover with a tight-fitting lid and simmer for 30 minutes or until the chicken is tender.

Transfer the chicken and onions to a warm serving dish. Turn up the heat and boil the sauce to reduce it slightly. Season to taste.

Spoon the sauce over the chicken and garnish with a sprinkling of spring onions. Serve hot.

SPICED BEAN CHICKEN

SERVES 4

175 g (6 oz) mixed dried pulses (red kidney beans, chick peas, haricot beans etc)

1 clove garlic, finely chopped

1 medium onion, finely chopped

30 ml (2 tbsp) vegetable oil

2.5 ml (½ tsp) turmeric

2.5 ml (½ tsp) ground cumin

8 medium chicken drumsticks

salt and freshly ground black pepper

6 tomatoes, seeded and chopped

600 ml (1 pt) chicken stock

100–125 g (4 oz) okra (ladies fingers)

Garnish

freshly chopped parsley

A feast of protein with an Eastern flavour, serve with some naan bread and a crisp fresh salad.

Soak the pulses in cold water overnight. Drain and put into a pan with enough fresh cold water to cover well, and boil steadily for 10 minutes. Drain thoroughly.

Heat the oil in a large saucepan, add the onion and garlic and cook gently until softened.

Add the spices and cook for a further minute then add the chicken drumsticks. Season to taste. Cook, stirring for 5 minutes until the chicken is coated with the spices.

Add the tomatoes, stock, and drained pulses, cover and simmer gently for 45–60 minutes or until the beans are tender.

Add the okra (ladies fingers) 5 minutes before the end of cooking.

Serve piping hot sprinkled with fresh chopped parsley.

BASIL FRIED CHICKEN
SERVES 4

Pound the green chilli and garlic together with a mortar and pestle or in a blender.

Heat the oil in a wok or pan, then add the chilli-garlic mixture. Fry for 1 minute. Add the chicken and stir-fry for 1 minute; then add the red chilli, oyster sauce, fish sauce and soya sauce. Stir-fry for 2 minutes, mix the basil in well and serve immediately.

Serve accompanied by rice.

INGREDIENTS

8 fresh green chillies, chopped lightly

8 garlic cloves, chopped lightly

50 ml (2 fl oz) peanut or corn oil

300 g (11 oz) boneless skinned minced chicken

2 fresh red chillies, quartered lengthwise

15 ml (1 tbsp) oyster sauce

2.5 ml (½ tsp) fish sauce

1.5 ml (¼ tsp) black soy sauce

20 g (¼ oz) sweet basil leaves

TROPICAL STIR-FRY

SERVES 4

INGREDIENTS

1 small onion, finely chopped

4 tbsp sunflower oil

1 clove garlic, crushed

2 boneless chicken breasts (approx. 175 g
(6 oz) each), skinned and cut into thin strips

15 ml (1 tbsp) sunflower seeds

40 g (1½ oz) salted cashew nuts

½ ripe, pink skinned mango, stoned and
thinly sliced

2 kiwi fruit, peeled and sliced

4 kumquats, halved

salt and freshly ground black pepper

30 ml/2 tbsp flaked coconut

The wonderful thing about stir-fry recipes is that any number or combination of ingredients can be used. Serve with plain boiled rice.

Stir-fry the onion in half the oil for 3 minutes. Add the remaining oil, garlic and the chicken and stir-fry briskly until the chicken is evenly coloured and almost tender.

Add the sunflower seeds and cashew nuts and stir-fry for a further minute. Add the mango, kiwi, kumquats and salt and pepper to taste. Stir fry for a further 2 to 3 minutes.

Sprinkle with flaked coconut and serve immediately.

CHICKEN KASHMIR
SERVES 4

INGREDIENTS

750 g (1½ lb) boneless chicken, cubed
(breast or thigh)
150 ml (¼ pt) natural yogurt
5 ml (1 tsp) ground coriander
5 ml (1 tsp) ground cumin
5 ml (1 tsp) ground cinnamon
2.5 ml (½ tsp) coriander (cilantro) seeds
2.5 ml (½ tsp) ground ginger
salt
15 ml (1 tbsp) vegetable oil
1 medium onion, sliced
1 clove garlic, finely chopped
15 ml (1 tbsp) plain (all purpose) flour
90 ml (6 tbsp) chicken stock (broth)
25 g (1 oz) creamed coconut
45 ml (3 tbsp) freshly chopped coriander
25 g (1 oz) flaked almonds, toasted, to
garnish

For those who like a milder, more subtle Indian dish, this is ideal. The selected spices are 'warm' rather than 'hot' and the sauce is creamy.

Cut the chicken into bite-size pieces. Place in a bowl with the yogurt, coriander, cumin, cinnamon, coriander seeds, ground ginger and a little salt and stir until well coated. Cover and chill for 4 hours, but preferably overnight.

Heat the oil in a pan, add the onion and garlic and sauté until softened and golden. Strain the chicken pieces and add to the pan. Sauté until sealed.

Sprinkle on the flour, then blend in the chicken stock (broth). Add the creamed coconut and stir until it dissolves and the mixture thickens.

Pour in the remaining yogurt and spice marinade. Cover and simmer for 25 minutes or until the chicken is tender. Adjust seasoning, if necessary.

Five minutes before the end, stir in the chopped coriander.

Serve the chicken, sprinkled with the toasted almonds and accompanied with rice.

SPANISH CHICKEN WITH TOMATOES, PEPPER AND CUMIN

SERVES 2

A simple, spicy summer lunch for two, this recipe originally comes from Spain.

Split the poussin, cutting the backbone free, and rub salt and pepper into the flesh. Heat the oil in a small casserole and colour the chicken on the skin side while you prepare the vegetables.

Add the onions, tomatoes and pepper as they are prepared, tucking in the backbone (if using a poussin) and bayleaf. Cover and cook over a low heat for 15–20 minutes.

Meanwhile, grind the cumin seeds in a mortar, working in the chopped garlic. Remove the backbone, stir the vegetables gently and work in the cumin paste.

Cook for another 3–4 minutes, to allow the flavours to blend. Serve with the chicken skin upwards.

INGREDIENTS

1 poussin, about 600 g (1½ lb), or 2 chicken legs

salt and freshly ground black pepper

30 ml (2 tbsp) olive oil

2 onions, chopped

4 large tomatoes, chopped

1 green pepper, seeded and chopped

2 bayleaves

5 ml (1 tsp) cumin seeds

2 garlic cloves, finely chopped

CHICKEN WITH SPRING ONIONS

SERVES 4

INGREDIENTS

375 g (12 oz) boneless chicken breasts, skinned

1 egg white

5 ml (1 tsp) cornflour

5 ml (1 tsp) salt

45 ml (3 tbsp) dry sherry

90 ml (6 tbsp) groundnut oil

50 g (2 oz) cashew nuts

50 g (2 oz) mushrooms, sliced (see Note)

50 g (2 oz) water chestnuts, halved

4 large spring onions (scallions), trimmed and sliced into 2.5 cm (1 in) lengths

15 ml (1 tbsp) soy sauce

4 spring onion tassles or curls to garnish (optional)

The dish is typical of many Chinese recipes – full of flavour, contrasting textures and colours and quickly prepared. Stir-frying ensures that the chicken juices are sealed in and very little goodness, nutritionally, is lost during cooking.

Cut the chicken in 1 cm (½ inch) cubes. Place in a bowl with the egg white, salt and 15 ml (1 tbsp) sherry and mix well.

Heat the oil in a large frying pan or wok, and stir-fry the chicken for 2 minutes. Transfer to absorbent kitchen paper to drain.

Pour off the oil, wipe the pan clean and return 15 ml (1 tbsp) oil to the pan.

Add the cashews, mushrooms, water chestnuts and half the spring onions to the hot oil. Stir-fry for 1 minute, then add the soy sauce and the rest of the sherry.

Return the chicken to the pan and stir-fry for another 2 minutes.

Serve immediately, sprinkled with the remaining spring onions and garnished with spring onions tassles or curls if desired.

NOTE

If Chinese mushrooms are used, first soak them for 15 minutes in warm water.

RED CHICKEN CURRY

SERVES 6

INGREDIENTS

1.25 l (40 fl oz) thin coconut milk

10 white peppercorns, crushed

300 g (11 oz) boneless skinned chicken breasts, cut across into 5 mm (¼ in) thick slices

45 ml (3 tbsp) fish sauce

8 ml (½ tbsp) palm sugar

7 small white aubergines (eggplants), quartered

3 fresh red chillies, quartered lengthwise

2 kaffir lime leaves, torn into small pieces

20 g (¼ oz) sweet basil leaves

Chilli Paste

5 dried red chillies, chopped roughly

7.5 ml (1½ tsp) shallots, sliced

8 ml (½ tbsp) lemon grass, finely sliced

8 ml (½ tbsp) chopped garlic

10 ml (2 tsp) salt

5 ml (1 tsp) shrimp paste

5 ml (1 tsp) ginger, sliced

2.5 ml (½ tsp) lime or lemon zest, chopped

2.5 ml (½ tsp) coriander root or stem, chopped

In Thailand this curry is served in bowls accompanied by rice, sun-dried beef, and salted preserved eggs.

Heat 225 ml (8 fl oz) of the coconut milk in a pan, stir in the chilli paste and white peppercorns, and cook for 2 minutes.

Add the chicken slices, mix well and add the rest of the coconut milk. Bring to a boil, then add the fish sauce and palm sugar.

Boil for 1 minute and then add the aubergine (eggplant), chilli and lime leaf. Bring back to the boil, cook for 3 minutes, add the basil, remove from the heat and serve.

YAKITORI CHICKEN SKEWERS

SERVES 2 OR 4

Mirin is available from Japanese food shops – but if you cannot obtain it, substitute with a dry sherry. Serve these skewers either as a starter, or with plain boiled rice as a main course. Chicken livers are sometimes included in Yakitori.

In a bowl mix together with garlic, ginger, soy sauce, rice wine, sake and sugar. Stir in the chicken cubes. Cover with cling film and leave to marinate for 1 to 2 hours.

Thread the chicken onto bamboo skewers 15–20 cm (6–8 in) long, alternating with the spring onions and mushrooms. Brush with the marinade and arrange under a preheated grill.

Cook for 8 to 10 minutes, basting frequently with the marinade, and turning the skewers several times, until the chicken is cooked through.

Serve immediately, garnished with cucumber slices.

NOTE

Soak bamboo skewers for 30 minutes before using to prevent them from burning.

INGREDIENTS

1 clove garlic, chopped

2.5 cm (1 in) piece fresh ginger, peeled and chopped

75 ml (5 tbsp) soy sauce

60 ml (4 tbsp) mirin (sweet rice wine) or dry sherry

60 ml (4 tbsp) sake

30 ml (2 tbsp) sugar

500 g (1 lb) boned and skinned chicken meat, cut into 2.5 cm (1 in) cubes

6–8 spring onions (scallions), trimmed and cut into 2.5 cm (1 in) lengths

175 g (6 oz) mushrooms, halved

½ cucumber, sliced, to garnish

TANGY LIME JUICE AND GARLIC CHICKEN WINGS

SERVES 6

Place the chicken wings in a shallow dish. Rub the crushed garlic all over the chicken wings, then season with salt and freshly ground black pepper.

Sprinkle the lime juice and cayenne pepper over the chicken wings, cover, and marinate in the refrigerator for 3–4 hours, turning and rearranging them occasionally.

Arrange the chicken wings in a large frying pan and pour the marinade over them. Add just enough cold water to cover the wings and bring quickly to the boil. Cook, uncovered, for 20–25 minutes, or until the chicken is cooked through and the sauce has reduced slightly. Serve warm or, better still, cold the next day.

INGREDIENTS

12 chicken wings

4 garlic cloves, crushed

salt and freshly ground black pepper, to taste

freshly squeezed juice of 4 limes

pinch of cayenne pepper

CHAPTER THREE

RICE AND PASTA

CHICKEN RISOTTO

■

NASIGORENG

■

BLUSHING CHICKEN LIVERS

■

PAELLA VALENCIANA

■

CHICKEN PILAF

■

PAPRIKA CHICKEN

■

MEXICAN RICE CHICKEN

■

CARIBBEAN CHICKEN AND RICE STEW

■

CHICKEN FRIED RICE WITH CHILLI FISH SAUCE

CHICKEN RISOTTO
SERVES 4 TO 6

INGREDIENTS

500 g (1 lb) boneless chicken breasts, skinned and cubed

30 ml (2 tbsp) sunflower oil

1 onion, finely sliced

2 cloves garlic, crushed

5 ml (1 tsp) dried oregano

250 g (9 oz) Arborio or long grain rice

15 ml (1 tbsp) tomato purée

1.2 l (2 pt) strong chicken stock

splash dry white wine

salt and freshly ground black pepper

6 tomatoes, skinned, deseeded and chopped

10 pitted black olives, halved

Garnish

30 ml (2 oz) Parmesan cheese, grated

A true Italian risotto uses Arborio rice, which contributes to the characteristic creamy texture. If you prefer a slightly wetter risotto, add a little more stock (or wine!).

Heat the oil in a large pan, and cook the onion and garlic over a gentle heat until softened. Add the chicken and cook until golden brown.

Add the oregano and rice and cook for a further minute, stirring well. Blend in the tomato purée, stock and wine. Season to taste and stir well.

Cook over a gentle heat for 25–30 minutes or until the liquid is absorbed, but the rice still has a nutty bite to it.

Lightly fork in the tomatoes, olives and chopped parsley or basil. Heat through for a further 2 minutes. Serve, sprinkled with the Parmesan cheese.

NASIGORENG

SERVES 4 TO 6

INGREDIENTS

250 g (9 oz) long grain rice
60 ml (4 tbsp) groundnut oil
2 onions, finely chopped
1 clove garlic, finely chopped
1 fresh red chilli, finely shredded
2 tomatoes, skinned, seeded and chopped
250 g (9 oz) cooked chicken, diced
175 g (6 oz) cooked prawns, coarsely chopped
salt and freshly ground black pepper
30 ml (2 tbsp) chopped fresh coriander

Omelette

15 ml (1 tbsp) groundnut oil
3 spring onions (scallions) finely chopped
salt and freshly ground black pepper
30 ml (2 tbsp) light soy sauce
4 eggs, beaten

Garnish

paprika
cucumber slices

Cook the rice until just tender. Drain thoroughly and spread out on a tray to cool.

Heat the oil in a large pan. Sauté the onions and garlic until softened and golden. Add the chilli and cook for a further 2 minutes.

Stir in the tomatoes, chicken and prawns. Cook for 2 minutes, then add the rice. Stir-fry until the rice turns a light golden colour. Season to taste. Stir in the fresh coriander.

Mound the rice mixture onto a platter, cover and keep warm.

For the omelette, heat the oil in a large frying pan. Add the spring onions and cook until softened.

Season with salt and pepper and add the soy sauce. Cook for a further 2 minutes.

Stir the beaten eggs into the pan. Cook over a low heat until the omelette is set.

Carefully remove the omelette from the pan onto a chopping board. Loosely roll and shred it finely.

Arrange the shreds of omelette over the rice. Sprinkle with a light dusting of paprika and garnish with cucumber slices. Serve immediately, with extra soy sauce and a selection of salads and relishes.

BLUSHING CHICKEN LIVERS

SERVES 4

Here the chicken livers are quickly cooked in a spicy tomato sauce. They are good served with jacket potatoes, creamed potatoes or noodles and a green salad.

Rinse the chicken livers and pat dry on absorbent kitchen paper towels.

Heat the butter and oil in a saucepan. Sauté the onions and garlic until lightly browned and softened.

Sprinkle in the chilli powder and stir in the chicken livers. Cook for 4 minutes.

Add the tomatoes and mushrooms and cook for a further minute. Then stir in the tomato purée, red wine or Marsala, herbs and Worcestershire sauce. Simmer, uncovered, for 4 minutes. The liquid will reduce a little.

Season to taste and stir in the fromage frais.

Serve immediately, garnished liberally with chopped parsley.

INGREDIENTS

500 g (1 lb) chicken livers
15 g (½ oz) butter
15 ml (1 tbsp) vegetable oil
1 large onion, diced
1 clove garlic, crushed
2.5 ml (½ tsp) hot chilli powder
3 tomatoes, peeled, deseeded and sliced
75 g (3 oz) button mushrooms, sliced
30 ml (2 tbsp) tomato purée
125 ml (4 fl oz) red wine or Marsala
2.5 ml (½ tsp) thyme, freshly chopped
pinch ground bayleaves
5 ml (1 tsp) Worcestershire sauce
salt and freshly ground black pepper
150 ml (¼ pt) fromage frais

Garnish

freshly chopped parsley

PAELLA VALENCIANA

SERVES 8

'Paella" is a traditional Spanish speciality, shared at celebrations and among friends. There are many local variations, but the essential ingredients are rice and saffron, with a choice of chicken, shellfish and vegetables. The word "paella" refers to the huge round shallow pan or "paelleras' this dish is cooked in, and because these pans could measure anything from 30 cm (12 in) to a metre (3 ft) across, they are usually placed on an open fire for cooking.

Joint the chicken, and then carefully chop into 5 cm (2 inch) squares, keeping the meat on the bones.

Place the carcass, together with the giblets and 170 ml/1¼ pints water, in a pan. Add any fish skin and bones and the herbs together with a little salt and pepper.

In a large pan, heat 30 ml (2 tablespoonfuls of this oil and brown the chicken all over, for about 10 minutes. Add the squid, cover and simmer for 10 minutes.

Add the onion and garlic and cook until soft and just turning golden.

Add the tomatoes. Simmer the mixture, uncovered, until the tomatoes have reduced to a pulp. This will take about 10 minutes.

Add the mussels and chorizo or sausage. Cover and cook for 2 to 3 minutes or until the mussels have opened. Remove the pan from the heat.

Heat the remaining oil in a paella pan or a large frying pan frying pan. When the oil is hot, add the rice and cook, stirring for 3 to 4 minutes.

Add the chicken mixture to the rice, together with the prawns, monkfish, peppers, beans, peas and mange tout, saffron (plus soaking liquid), paprika and salt. Cook, stirring, for 2 minutes.

Pour on 500 ml/18 fl oz of the strained stock. Bring to the boil, then reduce the heat immediately to a gentle simmer.

Cook for 15 to 20 minutes, shaking the pan from time to time (do not stir), and adding a little more stock if the mixture is drying out.

Five minutes before the end, add the unshelled prawns.

Garnish the paella with lemon wedges and freshly chopped parsley, and serve from the pan, accompanied with some good Spanish wine.

INGREDIENTS

1 × 1½ kg (31/2 lb) roasting chicken with giblets

90 ml (6 tbsp) sunflower oil

250 g (8 oz) squid, cleaned and chopped

2 large onions, chopped

2 large cloves garlic, chopped

1 bayleaf

1 sprig fresh thyme

200 g (7 oz) live mussels, scrubbed and debearded

200 g (7 oz) chorizo or other spicy sausage, cut into chunks

500 g (1 lb) Valencia or best risotto rice

175 g (6 oz) shelled prawns

250 g (8 oz) monkfish, cubed

1 sweet green (bell) pepper and 1 sweet red (bell) pepper, seeded and cut into 1 cm (1 in) pieces

175 g (6 oz) small French or green (string or snap) beans, top and tailed

75 g (3 oz) frozen peas (or 250 g (8 oz) peas in pod)

50 g (2 oz) mange tout, top and tailed

15 saffron strands, soaked in 30 ml (2 tbsp) hot water

10 ml (2 tsp) paprika

salt

Garnish

2 lemons

freshly chopped parsley

8 unshelled prawns

CHICKEN PILAF

SERVES 6 TO 8

INGREDIENTS

100 g (4 oz) butter
1 kg (2 lb) chicken breasts, skinned, boned
and cut into bite-sized pieces
salt and freshly ground black pepper, to
taste
pinch of ground cinnamon
pinch of ground allspice
2 onions, chopped
45 ml (3 tbsp) tomato purée
600 ml (1 pt) boiling water
225 g (8 oz) long-grain rice
50 g (2 oz) butter

Garnish

chopped fresh mint

The classic Greek way to finish preparing this dish, and also many others which use pasta or rice, is to brown some butter in a small pan and pour it over just before serving. It's an optional stage in this version, and if you are particularly worried about your fat intake you might like to leave it out.

Melt the butter in a large, heavy-based saucepan and sauté the chicken pieces for 5–10 minutes or until lightly browned, turning during cooking. Add the salt and freshly ground black pepper, cinnamon and allspice, and stir well.

Add the onions to the saucepan and continue to cook until softened. Stir in the tomato purée and boiling water.

Cover and cook for 20 minutes; then add the rice. Cover and continue to simmer for a further 20–25 minutes or until the chicken is cooked through and the rice is tender.

Remove the cover for the final 10 minutes of the cooking time to allow the liquid to be absorbed. Melt the butter in a small frying pan and cook until browned. Turn the pilaf out on to a warm serving platter and pour the browned butter over the top. Sprinkle with chopped fresh mint to serve.

PAPRIKA CHICKEN

SERVES 4

Paprika chicken uses, as the name implies, the subtle, milder dried red pepper – never to be confused or substituted for hotter members of the family like cayenne or chilli. Serve this warming dish with noodles or pasta shells.

Joint the chicken into 8 pieces, and remove the skin where possible.

Heat the oil in a large pan and sauté the chicken until browned. Remove and set aside. Add the onions to the pan and cook until softened.

Sprinkle in the paprika and cook for a further minute. Blend in the wine.

Return the chicken pieces to the pan together with the tomatoes, purée, pimentos (sweet red peppers), bouquet garni and salt to taste. Cover and simmer for 45 minutes.

Transfer the chicken to a serving dish to keep warm. Rub the contents of the pan through a sieve. Return to rinsed pan and reheat. Season to taste.

Swirl in the yoghurt and pour over the chicken pieces. Sprinkle with the chopped parsley. Serve immediately.

INGREDIENTS

15 kg (3½ lb) oven-ready chicken
30 ml (2 tbsp) vegetable oil
2 medium onions, peeled and thinly sliced
10 ml (2 tsp) paprika
100–125 ml (4 fl oz) dry white wine
450 g (1 lb) tomatoes, deseeded and chopped or 400 g (14 oz) can tomatoes
15 ml (1 tbsp) tomato purée
2 whole canned pimentos (sweet red pepper), roughly chopped
bouquet garni
salt ·
60 ml (4 tbsp) natural yoghurt

Garnish

15 ml (1 tbsp) chopped parsley

MEXICAN RICE CHICKEN

SERVES 6

This recipe adds chicken to authentic spicy Mexican or Spanish Rice.

Cut the chicken into serving pieces. Fry until golden; drain and set aside. In the same oil, fry the chopped or sliced onion together with the garlic. Drain, and add to the chicken, together with the tomatoes, stock and spices. Bring to the boil; simmer for about half an hour.

Meanwhile, still in the same oil – adding a little more if necessary – fry the rice until it is golden, stirring frequently. Add the rice to the chicken; mix well; bring back to the boil, stirring frequently.

When the rice has absorbed all the visible liquid (10–20 minutes), add the peas; stir briefly; then cover tightly and simmer over a very low heat for another 20 minutes or so.

INGREDIENTS

1.5–1.75 kg (3½–4 lb) chicken

2 medium onions, chopped finely

2 cloves garlic, chopped

2 serrano chillies, chopped (fresh or canned)

450 g (1 lb) peeled and de-seeded tomatoes or 1 can tomatoes

50 ml (2 fl oz) olive oil

450 g (1 lb) long-grain rice

1.5 ml (¼ tsp) whole cumin seed

1.5 ml (¼ tsp) saffron

900 ml (1½ pt) chicken stock

salt and pepper

200 g (7 oz) peas, fresh or frozen

CARIBBEAN CHICKEN AND RICE STEW

SERVES 6

This tasty chicken stew comes from Puerto Rico.

Mix the garlic, oregano, and salt together in a large bowl. Add the chicken pieces, and mix them well together. Heat the butter or margarine in a saucepan, and brown the chicken pieces. Transfer them to a plate.

Add the onion and green peppers to the pan, and cook until soft.

Add the tomatoes and browned chicken pieces, coating them well with the onion, peppers, and tomato mixture. Reduce the heat and simmer for 30 minutes, or until the chicken is cooked.

Remove the chicken to a plate and leave to cool a little.

Remove the bones, and cut the flesh into 5 cm (2 in) pieces.

Meanwhile, add the rice, stock and freshly ground black pepper to the onion, peppers and tomato mixture, and bring to the boil. Reduce the heat, cover, and simmer for 20 minutes or until the rice is cooked.

Stir in the peas, Parmesan, and hot pepper. Mix well, then add the chicken. Cover and simmer for 2 more minutes, then serve.

INGREDIENTS

1 garlic clove, chopped
2.5 ml (½ tsp) dried oregano
2.5 ml (½ tsp) salt
1.5 kg (3½ lb) chicken, cut into 8 pieces
60 ml (4 tbsp) butter or margarine
1 small onion, finely chopped
150 g (5 oz) green peppers, chopped
4 ripe tomatoes, skinned and chopped
350 g (12 oz) uncooked long-grain white rice
2.25 l (3¼ pt) chicken stock
freshly ground black pepper
450 g (1 lb) frozen peas
50 g (2 oz) Parmesan cheese, freshly grated
1 fresh hot pepper, chopped

CHICKEN FRIED RICE WITH CHILLI FISH SAUCE

SERVES 4

Heat the oil in a wok or pan, add the chicken and garlic and mix well over the heat for 1 minute. add the onion and cook for 1 minute, break in the eggs, mix very well and then stir in the rice and the rest of the ingredients. Stir well. Cook for 2 minutes and serve immediately.

To make the chilli fish sauce, mix all the ingredients together well.

Serve the fried rice accompanied by cucumber slices, whole spring onions and the Chilli Fish sauce.

INGREDIENTS

45 ml (3 tbsp) peanut or corn oil
200g (7oz) boneless skinned chicken breasts, cut lenghtwise into 1cm (½ in) thick slices
15 ml (1 tbsp) chopped garlic
1 medium-sized onion, sliced
2 eggs
15 ml (1 tbsp) chopped garlic
750g (1¼ lb) cooked rice
1 tomato, cut into 8 wedges
1 spring onion (scallion), chopped
10 ml (2 tsp) white soy sauce
5 ml (1 tsp) commercially available fish sauce
5 ml (1tsp) sugar
5 ml (1tsp) ground white pepper

Chilli Fish sauce
50 ml (2 floz) fish sauce
10 fresh small green chillis, sliced into small circles
5 ml (1 tsp) sliced shallot
1.5 ml (¼ tsp) sugar
15 ml (1 tbsp) lime or lemon juice

CHAPTER FOUR

ROASTS, STEWS AND CASSEROLES

PARMESAN BAKED CHICKEN

◾

FRAGRANT CHICKEN PARCELS

◾

MUSCAT BAKED ALMOND CHICKEN

◾

ARMENIAN STYLE CHICKEN AND CHICKPEA STEW

◾

COUNTRY CHICKEN HOTPOT

◾

CARIBBEAN CHICKEN CASSEROLE

◾

GARDEN CHICKEN

◾

FARMYARD CHICKEN WITH OLIVES

◾

CALYPSO CHICKEN

◾

TOMATO AND CHICKEN CASSEROLE

◾

SOUTHERN STUFFED CHICKEN THIGHS

PARMESAN BAKED CHICKEN

SERVES 4

INGREDIENTS

4 boneless chicken breasts, approx. 150 g
(5 oz) each
30 ml (2 tbsp) olive oil
2 medium onions, finely chopped
2 cloves garlic, finely chopped
1 stick celery, chopped
425 g (14 oz) can chopped tomatoes
15 ml (1 tbsp) tomato purée
few drops Tabasco
5 ml (1 tsp) fresh basil, chopped
5 ml (1 tsp) fresh oregano, chopped
5 ml (1 tsp) sugar
30 ml (2 tbsp) lemon juice
1 egg, beaten
25 g (1 oz) plain four, seasoned
150 g (6 oz) Mozzarella cheese, grated
30 ml (2 tbsp) grated Parmesan cheese
salt and freshly ground black pepper

Garnish

fresh watercress

Heat half the oil in a pan and sauté the onions, garlic and celery until softened. Stir in the tomatoes, purée, Tabasco. herbs and sugar. Season with salt and pepper. Simmer, uncovered, for 25–30 minutes.

Sprinkle the skinned chicken breasts with lemon juice. Dip each breast into the egg and then the seasoned flour. Shake off any excess.

Heat the remaining oil in a non-stick frying pan and sauté the chicken breasts for 5 minutes, turning halfway through, until golden brown. Drain on absorbent kitchen paper towel.

Lay the chicken in an ovenproof dish and cover with half the Mozzarella cheese. Pour over sauce, top with the remaining cheese, and sprinkle with Parmesan.

Bake for 25–30 minutes at 180°C/ 350°F/Gas 5 or until bubbling and golden.

Serve, garnished with fresh watercress.

FRAGRANT CHICKEN PARCELS

INGREDIENTS

5 ml (1 tsp) cornflour
grated rind ½ lemon
45 ml (3 tbsp) natural yoghurt
3 cardamom pods, seeds only, crushed
2.5 ml (½ tsp) coriander seeds, crushed
15 ml (1tbsp) freshly chopped chervil
10 ml (2 tsp) freshly chopped tarragon
10 ml (2tsp) dijon mustard
salt and freshly ground pepper
4 boneless chicken breasts, approx. 175g
(6 oz), skinned

Garnish

lemon juice
fresh chervil

In a shallow dish, blend together the first nine ingredients. Make a couple of slashes in the chicken breasts, then coat the chicken with the sauce. Leave in the dish, cover and marinate for 2–3 hours in a cool place.

Place each breast in the centre of a large piece of foil. Spoon over any remaining marinade. Wrap the foil up around the chicken, making sure you seal it well.

Cook for 20–25 minutes at 190°C/ 375°F/Gas 6 or until the chicken is tender. Serve the chicken in the foil parcels, opened up and garnish it with lemon slices and fresh chervil.

MUSCAT BAKED ALMOND CHICKEN

SERVES 6

Wash and pat dry the chicken, rub it all over with salt and pepper to taste, the cinnamon and the nutmeg. Take 2–3 sprigs of lemon thyme and the same of oregano and put them inside the chicken. Place it in a casserole, stuff with half the grapes and pour over the wine. Cover and cook the chicken in a preheated 200°C/400°F/Gas 6 oven for 1½ hours.

Remove the chicken from the oven and transfer it to a warm serving platter. Remove the grapes and herbs from the cavity, joint the chicken and cover it with foil to keep it warm.

In a small saucepan, melt the butter and sauté the sliced almonds for a few minutes until just coloured. Remove with a slotted spoon and set aside. Skim the fat from the chicken cooking juices in the casserole and strain them into the saucepan. Heat the juices gently until very hot, but not boiling, and stir in the remaining grapes and the ground almonds. Allow to cook for a few minutes to combine.

In a small bowl beat the cream and egg yolks together lightly. Take a spoonful of the hot chicken stock and stir it into the egg. Remove the saucepan from the heat and stir in the egg mixture; the sauce should thicken as you stir.

Pour some of the sauce over the jointed chicken and sprinkle it with the toasted almonds. Pour the remainder into a sauceboat to be served with pilau rice.

INGREDIENTS

2 kg (4½ lb) free-range chicken
salt and freshly ground pepper
2.5 ml (½ tsp) cinnamon
large pinch nutmeg
fresh lemon thyme
fresh oregano
225 g (8 oz) muscat grapes, skinned, seeded and halved
250 ml (8 fl oz) sweet muscat wine
15 ml (1 tbsp) butter
45 ml (3 tbsp) sliced blanched almonds
50 g (2 oz) ground almonds
salt and freshly ground pepper
150 ml (5 fl oz) single cream
2 egg yolks

ARMENIAN-STYLE CHICKEN AND CHICKPEA STEW

SERVES 6

INGREDIENTS

4 threads saffron

125 ml (4 fl oz) hot water

10 cloves garlic, crushed

2 fresh thin medium-hot red peppers, seeded and chopped

60 ml (4 tbsp) vegetable or sunflower oil

1.3 kg (3 lb) chicken breasts and thighs, washed and dried

salt and freshly ground black pepper

30 ml (2 tbsp) ground coriander

5 ml (1 tsp) dried oregano

2 × 400 g (14 oz) cans plum tomatoes, drained

480 ml (16 fl oz) water

600 g (1¼ lb) can chickpeas, drained

30 ml (2 tbsp) lemon juice

Soak the saffron in hot water for 10 minutes. Place the saffron and liquid, garlic and peppers in a blender or food processor. Process until finely chopped and set aside.

Heat the oil in a casserole over medium-hot heat. Season the chicken to taste, and sauté in batches until lightly browned. Remove to a plate and keep warm.

Reduce the heat and add the crushed garlic. Stir with a wooden spoon for 2 minutes, then add the ground coriander and oregano. Stir for a further 2 minutes, then add the tomatoes. Break them up with the spoon while cooking for 3 minutes, then add the water. Add the chicken pieces and spoon the sauce over them. Bring to the boil, cover, and simmer over low heat for 20 minutes.

Add the chickpeas and continue to cook, covered, for a further 15 minutes. Remove the lid, stir in the lemon juice, and increase the heat. Boil for 5 minutes to reduce the sauce. Serve immediately.

COUNTRY CHICKEN HOTPOT

SERVES 4

INGREDIENTS

4 medium sized potatoes

2 large carrots, peeled and chopped

3 sticks celery, chopped

175 g (6 oz) shredded green cabbage

4 chicken legs (approx. 175 g (6 oz) each)

25 g (1 oz) seasoned flour

30 ml (2 tbsp) vegetable oil

15 ml (1 tbsp) fresh thyme, chopped

salt and freshly ground black pepper

300 ml (½ pt) beef stock (broth)

150 ml (¼ pt) Guinness or stout

15 ml (1 tbsp) dark soft brown sugar

1 egg, beaten

chopped fresh thyme, to garnish

Reminiscent of the Irish hot pot, made even more authentic by the addition of some Irish stout!

Peel the potatoes; cut two of the potatoes into thin slices, and chop the other two.

Mix the chopped potato with the carrot, celery and cabbage.

Dust the chicken legs with seasoned flour. Heat the oil in a large pan and sauté the chicken legs until lightly golden on all sides. Add the thyme, and salt and pepper to taste.

Place half of the mixed vegetables in the base of a deep casserole. Top with the chicken legs and then the remaining vegetables.

Mix the stock (broth), Guinness or stout and brown sugar together and pour over the contents of the casserole.

Overlap the potato slices in concentric circles on top of the vegetables and chicken. Brush with a little oil.

Cover with a piece of lightly oiled foil and cook at 350°F for 1 hour.

Remove the foil. Brush the potato crust with the beaten egg. Return to the oven for a further 35 to 40 minutes. Serve sprinkled with chopped thyme.

CARIBBEAN CHICKEN CASSEROLE

SERVES 6

Wash the chicken. Marinate the pieces in a bowl with the salt, pepper, garlic, thyme, bayleaf, and vinegar for 5 hours.

Heat the oil in a large saucepan, then add the tomatoes and chicken pieces. Cover with cold water, bring it to the boil, then lower the heat and simmer, covered, for 30 minutes or until the chicken is almost cooked and the liquid has reduced.

Add the onion and the other vegetables, and cook until they are tender but crisp.

Serve immediately with fresh bread or boiled rice and hot pepper sauce.

INGREDIENTS

1.5 kg (3½ lb) chicken, cut into 5 cm (2 in) pieces
5 ml (1 tsp) salt
5 ml (1 tsp) freshly ground black pepper
2 garlic cloves
1.5 ml (¼ tsp) chopped fresh thyme
10 ml (2 tsp) vinegar
1 bayleaf
30 ml (2 tbsp) vegetable oil
1 medium tomato, chopped
2 celery sticks, chopped
2 carrots, diced
¼ cabbage, shredded
4 potatoes, chopped
175 g (6 oz) green beans, cleaned

57

GARDEN CHICKEN

SERVES 6

INGREDIENTS

1 x 1.5 kg (3½ lb) oven-ready chicken
sprigs of fresh herbs
wedge of lemon
salt and freshly ground black pepper
60 ml (4 tbsp) vegetable oil
2 medium onions, sliced
1 large clove garlic, chopped
1 aubergine (eggplant), cubed
3 medium potatoes, cubed
125 g (4 oz) green (string or snap) beans
1 sweet red (bell) pepper, deseeded
and sliced
1 sweet green (bell) pepper, deseeded
and sliced
175 g (6 oz) courgettes cut into chunks
125 g (4 oz) button mushrooms
1.2 l (2 pt) chicken stock (broth)

Garnish

30 ml (2 tbsp) chopped walnuts
15 ml (1 tbsp) chopped fresh herbs

A wholesome 'hot pot' with an abundance of fresh vegetables. Accompany with wholemeal pasta, such as tagliatelle.

Open up the cavity of the chicken and put the sprigs of herbs and the lemon in the centre. Season inside and out with salt and pepper. Place the chicken in a large pan or flameproof casserole.

Heat the oil in a pan; add the onion and garlic and cook gently for 2 to 3 minutes. Add these to the chicken together with the remaining vegetables and the stock (broth).

Bring to the boil and simmer the chicken and vegetables gently in a covered pan for 1½ hours.

Spring with the nuts and chopped herbs and serve either straight from the casserole, or lift the chicken out onto a serving dish and surround with the cooked vegetables.

NOTE
If you like really crunchy vegetables then cook the chicken in the stock (broth) with the aubergine and add remaining vegetables during the last 30 minutes cooking time.

FARMYARD CHICKEN WITH OLIVES

SERVES 4

INGREDIENTS

1.25 kg (2¼ lb) corn fed chicken, quartered and backbone freed

2 onions, chopped

30 ml (2 tbsp) olive oil

3 garlic cloves, chopped

salt and freshly ground black pepper

24 green olives

175 ml (6 fl oz) fino sherry or Montilla

2 bayleaves

Fry the onions in the oil in a casserole, adding the garlic when they soften. Salt and pepper the chicken portions and pack these neatly into the pan, with the backbone, putting the olives in the spaces. Add the fino and bayleaves and pour in water to almost cover (about 350 ml (12 fl oz)). Simmer, covered, for 30–35 minutes.

Spoon the chicken from the casserole, allow to cool for a few minutes. Remove the bones and skin. Return these to the liquid and boil for a further 10 minutes. Check the seasonings.

Meanwhile split the cooked chicken into large pieces, arrange them in a shallow dish and distribute the olives. Strain the juices into a bowl and skim off all fat. Pour over the chicken and chill until set.

CALYPSO CHICKEN

SERVES 6

Wash the chicken in cold running water, rubbing with the lemon. Season with the salt, pepper, one of the cloves of garlic, crushed, plus the vinegar and thyme. Leave to marinate for about 3 hours.

In a large saucepan, melt the butter or margarine, then add the sugar. When it is bubbling, add the chicken and brown the pieces.

Meanwhile, in a frying pan, heat some oil. Fry half the cashews, then set them aside. In the same pan, fry together the remaining clove of garlic, crushed, the mushrooms, the other half of the cashews, onions and ginger. Add ¼ cup water, and pour the mixture into the large saucepan over the chicken. Cook for 25 minutes or until the chicken is cooked.

Thicken with the flour mixed with some warm water and stirred into the chicken mixture. Cook for 3 more minutes, then sprinkle with the remaining fried cashews.

Serve with boiled rice.

INGREDIENTS

1.3 kg (3 lb) chicken, cut into 5 cm (2 in) pieces
½ lemon
10 ml (2 tsp) salt
freshly ground black pepper
2 garlic cloves
15 ml (1 tbsp) vinegar
1.5 ml (¼ tsp) chopped fresh thyme
30 ml (2 tbsp) butter or margarine
10 ml (2 tsp) brown sugar
oil for frying
225 g (8 oz) cashew nuts
100–125 g (4 oz) mushrooms, sliced
3 onions, chopped
6 slices fresh root ginger
15 ml (1 tbsp) plain flour

TOMATO AND CHICKEN CASSEROLE

SERVES 4 TO 6

Preheat the oven to 190°C/375°F/Gas 5. Heat the oil in a large, flameproof casserole. Place the chicken portions on a chopping board and dredge all over with flour. Place in the casserole and cook for about 5 minutes, or until evenly browned, turning the portions as they cook. Using a slotted spoon, transfer the chicken portions to a plate and set aside.

Add the onion to the casserole and cook for 3 minutes, or until softened.

Return the chicken to the casserole, add the chopped tomatoes and garlic and season with salt and freshly ground black pepper. Add the boiling water, cover and cook in the oven for 45–55 minutes or until the chicken is tender and the sauce has thickened.

In the last 5 minutes of cooking time, stir in the red wine vinegar and a little extra boiling water if necessary. Serve sprinkled with chopped fresh parsley.

INGREDIENTS

50 ml (2 fl oz) olive oil

1.5 kg (3½ lb) prepared chicken, cut into portions

flour, for dredging

2 large red onions, sliced

2 × 400 g (14 oz) cans chopped tomatoes

3 garlic cloves, crushed

salt and freshly ground black pepper, to taste

75 ml (3 fl oz) boiling water

30 ml (2 tbsp) red wine vinegar

Garnish

chopped fresh parsley

SOUTHERN STUFFED CHICKEN THIGHS

SERVES 4

INGREDIENTS

15 ml (1 tbsp) olive oil

25 g (1 oz) onion, chopped

25 g (1 oz) celery, chopped

150 g (5 oz) uncooked chicken livers, finely chopped

1.5 ml (¼ tsp) ground ginger

1.5 ml (¼ tsp) salt

pinch of pepper

100–125 g (4 oz) soft breadcrumbs

1 green cooking apple, peeled, cored and cut into 5 mm (¼ in) dice

50 g (2 oz) walnuts, coarsely chopped

60–75 ml (4–5 tbsp) melted butter

45 ml (3 tbsp) milk

8 chicken thighs

2.5 ml (½ tsp) paprika

In a medium frying pan, sauté the onion and celery in the olive oil for 3 minutes. Add the chopped liver. Cook, stirring frequently, until liver is thoroughly browned, about 5 minutes. Add ginger, salt and pepper, and mix well.

In a medium bowl, mix breadcrumbs, apple and walnuts. Add the liver mixture. Add 30 ml (2 tablespoons) melted butter and enough milk so that stuffing is thoroughly moistened but not mushy.

Preheat oven to 180°C/350°F/Gas 4. Lightly grease a shallow 23 x 23 cm (9 x 9 in) (or slightly larger) baking dish. Trim excess skin and fat from chicken thighs. Remove bone by cutting thighs almost in half along the bone. Cut out the bone with a sharp knife. Place the boned thighs skin side down and spread out so you have a flat rectangle of meat. Place about 2 tablespoons of stuffing along the centre of each thigh. Roll up and fasten with wooden cocktail sticks or tie with string. Push any spilled stuffing back into roll and place in baking dish, rolled edges up.

Mix 30–45 ml (2 to 3 tbsp) melted butter and paprika. Brush butter over thighs. Lightly sprinkle with salt, if desired. Bake at 180°C/350°F/Gas 4, occasionally basting with pan juices, until chicken is cooked through, 50–60 minutes.